WORLD WAR II

TOM McGOWEN

WORLD
WAR II

FRANKLIN WATTS

New York ★ Chicago ★ London ★ Sydney

A First Book

For Grant

Photographs copyright ©: Imperial War Museum, London, cover, 18, 20 (bottom), 24, 39; Culver Pictures, 6, 10 (top), 27 (top); UPI/Bettmann, 9, 10 (bottom), 20 (top), 27 (bottom), 30, 36, 41 (bottom), 43 (top), 48, 51 (top); Brown Brothers, 15, 59; Sovfoto, 25, 41 (top); Naval Photographic Center, 29; The Bettmann Archive, 34, 43 (bottom), 45, 47, 54 (top & bottom right), 57; The National Archives, 51 (bottom); AP/Wide World, 53; U.S. Army 54 (bottom left).

Library of Congress Cataloging-in-Publication Data

McGowen, Tom.
World War II / Tom McGowen.
p. cm. — (A First book)
Includes bibliographical references and index.
Summary: Provides an overview of the military battles and political changes that occurred during World War II.
ISBN 0-531-20150-3 (HC : library binding)
ISBN 0-531-15661-3 (PB)
1. World War, 1939–1945—Juvenile literature. [1. World War, 1939–1945.] I. Title. II. Title: World War Two. III. Title: World War 2. IV. Series.
D743.7.M37 1993
940.53—dc20
92-28328 CIP AC

CONTENTS

German army tanks and supply wagons rumble into Poland,
marking the beginning of World War II.

ONE

1939

★

ON SEPTEMBER 1, 1939, the gray tanks and gray-clad troops of the German Army poured across the border of Poland, and World War II, history's most terrible war, began.

The main cause of World War II actually went back twenty-one years to Germany's surrender that ended World War I. By 1918, Germany was racked by riots, revolution, unemployment, and starvation, and facing invasion and occupation by the armies of France, Great Britain, and the United States. But the surrender terms were harsh. Germany was forced to give up large parts of its territory, had to agree to pay an enormous amount of money to France, had to give up its air force and navy and limit its army to only 100,000 men, and had to state officially that it had been guilty of starting the war. All of these things were bitterly resented by the German people. In the years following the war's end, a number of political groups made attempts to take over the German government, and one of these, the National Socialist German Workers Party, known as the

Nazi Party, denounced the surrender terms, preached that Germany had lost the war because it had been betrayed by traitors, and pledged to restore Germany to the power and armed might it had once possessed. This appealed to many Germans, and the Nazis gained in strength and popularity. In 1933 their leader, Adolf Hitler, an Austrian-born war veteran who had served in the German Army, was appointed Chancellor (Prime Minister) of Germany. He quickly made himself all-powerful and began to eliminate freedom in Germany and to wipe out all opposition and all people of whom he disapproved, chiefly Jews and communists. Hitler was ruthless, reckless, and dreamed of making Germany the ruling nation of the world, and he embarked on a program to rebuild the military and regain land lost by Germany as a result of the war. By 1936, ignoring the World War I surrender terms, Germany's army was 500,000 strong, it had an air force, and it was building a navy.

The Kingdom of Italy, although it had been on the winning side, had been badly weakened and humiliated by World War I, in which it lost many battles and finally had to be rescued by the French and British. Soon after the war, a political party known as the Fascists seized power, and their leader, Benito Mussolini, became Italy's Prime Minister. Like Hitler, Mussolini curtailed freedom, ruthlessly exterminating all opposition, and began building up his nation's army, navy, and air force, intent upon making Italy a formidable and feared power. Because of their similar views and

Adolf Hitler (standing in car) receives the Nazi salute from thousands of his followers in a parade prior to the outbreak of the war.

Leaders of the Axis nations: (Above), Benito Mussolini of Italy (left) and Adolf Hitler of Germany; at left, Emperor Hirohito of Japan.

political systems, he and Hitler signed a pact between their two nations in 1936, forming what was known as "the Rome-Berlin Axis."

The Empire of Japan had not fought any battles during World War I, but it had gained some territory as a result of being on the winning side, and its government was eager to gain more, for expansion. In 1931, a Japanese army invaded Manchuria, the northernmost province of China, which was rich in coal and iron, and in 1933 another Chinese province, Jehol, was taken over. In 1936, Japan signed a treaty with Germany and Italy, becoming part of the "Axis."

In the last half of the 1930s, Germany, Italy, and Japan grew ever more warlike. In 1935, Italy invaded the African nation of Ethiopia, intent upon making it a colony. In 1936, Germany retook the region known as the Rhineland, which had been separated from it as part of the World War I surrender terms. In 1937, Japanese forces pushed down into northern China. In the remaining two years of the decade Germany took over Austria and Czechoslovakia, while Italy invaded and quickly conquered the little Eastern European country of Albania. France and Great Britain, the two major powers then, did nothing to prevent any of these things, fearing that if they did, a major war would result. In the United States, many people were "Isolationists," believing that America should stay out of European affairs.

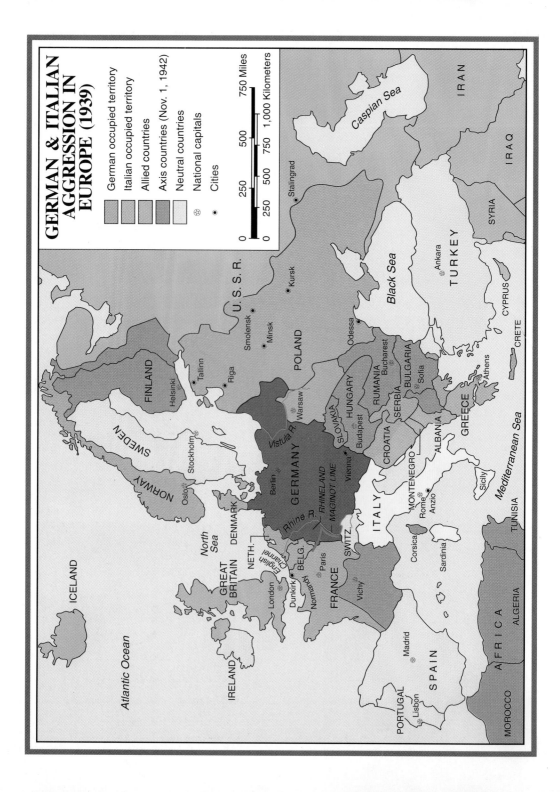

U.S.S.R.

*Kamchatka
Peninsula*

MONGOLIA

MANCHURIA

Sakhalin

Harbin

Kurile Islands

JEHOL Mukden
Peking *Yalu R.* Vladivostok

Hokkaido

KOREA

Honshu

C H I N A

JAPAN

Nagoya Tokyo
Kobe *Tokyo Bay*
Hiroshima Yokohama

Nagasaki *Shikoku*
Kyushu

Shanghai

Fu-chow *Okinawa*

Ryukyu Islands

Iwo Jima

B U R M A

Canton

Hong Kong *Taiwan*

Rangoon Hanoi

Hainan

*Pacific
Ocean*

THAILAND

Luzon

Bangkok

FRENCH
INDO-CHINA

*SOUTH
CHINA
SEA*

Manila

Saipan

Saigon

Guam

Palawan

P H I L I P P I N E S

NORTH
BORNEO
BRUNEI

*Palau
Islands*

M A L A Y A

Mindanao

SARAWAK

Singapore

Equator

Sumatra

Borneo

Celebes

NEW GUINEA

*INDIAN
OCEAN*

DUTCH EAST INDIES

JAPANESE AGGRESSION IN THE PACIFIC (1941)

0   250   500   750 Miles

0   500   1,000 Kilometers

Japanese territory
by 1941

⊛ National capitals

• Cities

In 1939, Hitler signed a peace treaty with the Soviet Union (Russia, the Ukraine, and most of today's Commonwealth of Independent States, which were then all under a single communist government). This eliminated the danger of war with the Soviet Union, and left Hitler free to make his next move, to invade Poland. France and Great Britain now finally acted, demanding that Germany withdraw its troops or they would declare war. Hitler virtually ignored them, and two days later they announced their declarations of war against Germany.

Poland had only a tiny air force, few tanks, and a large part of its army was made up of old-fashioned horsed cavalry, no match at all for Germany's tank divisions and dive bombers. By September 17, most of the Polish army had been destroyed, and on that day, as had been agreed in the treaty with Germany, the Soviet Union invaded Poland from the east. Poland was divided up between its two invaders.

Meanwhile, French and British troops were moving into position behind the Maginot Line, a string of steel and concrete fortifications running along the French border from Belgium down to Switzerland. With the exception of some battles between British and German warships in the North Sea and Atlantic Ocean, the remainder of the year was a period of so-called "phony war," with British and French troops sitting quietly behind the Maginot Line and German forces sitting behind their own string of fortifications along the German border, the Siegfried Line.

An entrance to the Maginot Line, the 125-mile (201-km) long row of
fortifications that France depended on to block a German invasion.

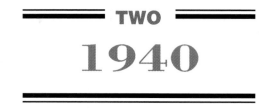

TWO

1940

★

THE ARMIES that began World War II were basically formed of units called divisions. An infantry (foot soldier) division consisted of 17,000 to 18,000 men armed with rifles, machine guns, small cannons called anti-tank guns that fired projectiles capable of piercing tank armor, and large artillery cannons that fired explosive projectiles for 9 miles (14.5km) or more. There were also armored divisions, formed of two hundred to three hundred and fifty tanks plus infantry and artillery. (The German army was far ahead of all others in the number of armored divisions it had and the way they were organized.) Two or three divisions of various kinds were grouped together to form a corps (pronounced *kor*), several corps were grouped together to form an army, and several armies formed an army group.

The major nations all had large air forces composed of fleets of bombers and squadrons of fighter planes (here, too, Germany was far ahead of most others). Navies were composed mainly of battleships, cruisers, and destroyers, which were all really just large armored platforms for enormous long-range cannons, but most navies also had aircraft carriers and large numbers of submarines armed mainly with torpedoes. There were no such things as helicopter gunships, jet airplanes, or guided missiles at this time.

The "phony war" came to a sudden end on April 9, 1940, when German forces swiftly invaded Denmark and Norway, to gain seaports and airbases for use against Britain. One month later, German armies struck into Holland and Belgium and German panzer (armor) divisions rolled through the Belgian Ardennes Forest—which French generals had believed could not be done—and came down into France behind the Maginot Line. British and French forces could not withstand the Blitzkrieg ("lightning war") tactics of the panzer divisions, in which dive bombers attacked troops on roads and in towns and fortresses, pinning them down so that tanks and motorcycle troops could come rushing upon them.

It became clear that France would soon be conquered, and the British government moved to get its army out of the country before it could be captured or wiped out, leaving Britain helpless. British army units began to withdraw toward the northern coast, where warships and hundreds of boats of all kinds, scraped up from all over Britain, were gathering off the small French port city of Dunkirk to take the British soldiers to safety. For twelve days, thousands of men stood on the beaches, waiting their turn to board a vessel, while German forces slowly closed around the area and

This painting depicts the evacuation of British and French troops from Dunkirk, under attack from German artillery and airplanes. 338,000 men were safely rescued and taken to Britain on ships that ranged from warships of the British Navy to small fishing boats and even rowboats.

both ships and beach were steadily bombed by German planes and shelled by artillery. But in what became known as "the Miracle of Dunkirk," 338,000 British and French troops were rescued and taken to Britain.

Meanwhile, the panzer divisions continued to destroy French forces, and on June 10, Germany's Axis partner, Italy, also invaded France. By the 25th France had surrendered and Britain stood alone, facing invasion.

The British leader, Prime Minister Winston Churchill, was a stocky, vigorous man who had been an officer in the British Army, a newspaper reporter, and had held several positions in the British government. He spoke to the British people on radio, warning them that they now faced a time of "blood, toil, tears, and sweat." Churchill's courage and fighting spirit made Britain firmly determined to never give up.

Throughout August and September the Battle of Britain was fought, as thousands of German air raids attacked airfields and factories in England and Scotland in an attempt to destroy Britain's fighter plane force and make things easier for an invasion. But although the British Royal Air Force fighter planes were greatly outnumbered by those of the German Luftwaffe, the British had three advantages. Their planes were slightly better; they had a chain of radar stations all around the coastline, which spotted German planes before they ever reached Britain; and they had deciphered the German radio code, so that they knew exactly

Right, a bombed out area of London after a German air raid during the night. Below, Italian prisoners of war captured by the British after the disastrous Italian invasion of Egypt.

when attacks were being launched. Thus, British planes were always able to meet an enemy attack with a maximum of strength at any point. By the end of September the Germans had lost 1,733 aircraft to 915 British planes, so the raids against military targets were halted and the planned invasion was called off by Hitler. However, in an attempt to batter the British people into a desire for peace, the Germans began nighttime bombing raids against Britain's cities, chiefly London. These air raids continued well into 1941.

Britain received food and raw materials from its colonies of India and Burma by ships that moved through the Suez Canal in eastern Egypt and then up through the Mediterranean Sea. Therefore, control of the canal and the sea was vital. In September, an Italian army moved out of the Italian colony of Libya into Egypt, with the goal of capturing the canal and cutting Britain's lifeline. In October, another Italian army struck out of Albania into Greece.

But Italy's confident moves brought it disaster. In Egypt, a British army smashed the Italians, taking 38,000 prisoners and driving the rest back into Libya, while the Greek army pushed the invaders back into Albania. British navy bombers inflicted a crippling blow on the Italian Mediterranean fleet, sinking five warships and critically damaging another. The focus of the war had suddenly shifted to North Africa and the Mediterranean Sea.

THREE
1941

★

THROUGHOUT January and February the British armies in North Africa scored victories, destroying the Italian force that had fled out of Egypt and invading the Italian possessions of Ethiopia and Italian Somaliland (now the southern part of Somalia). With things going so well, many British troops were pulled out of North Africa during February and March and sent across the Mediterranean Sea to aid Greece in its war against Italy. On March 17, an Italian naval force attempting to stop such a troop movement was intercepted by a group of British warships, and in a quick battle lost two cruisers and four destroyers. The remaining Italian ships fled back to port and the Italian fleet never ventured out to sea again. The British Navy now dominated the Mediterranean and the British Army seemed in full control of Africa.

The British, however, were suddenly faced with a new enemy in North Africa. Hitler saw the need to rescue his Italian allies, and on March 12 the first portion of the German panzer force known as the Afrika Korps landed at the port of Tripoli in western Libya, the last Italian strong-

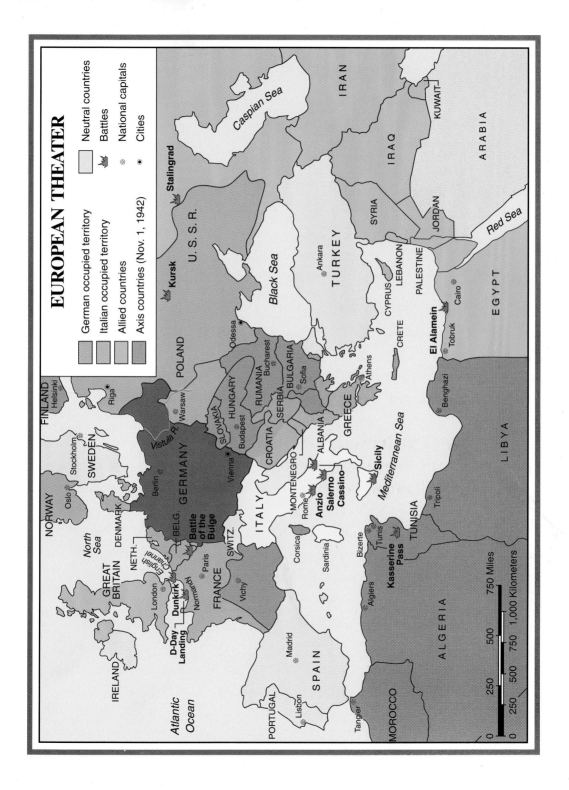

British Crusader tanks in action against the German Afrika Korps
in the Libyan desert, 1941.

hold. Its commander, General Erwin Rommel, recognized
that the British were weakened by sending so many troops
to Greece, and he lashed out in a quick, hard-hitting attack
that pushed the British back toward Egypt.

On April 6, German armies invaded Greece and
neighboring Yugoslavia. Within twelve days Yugoslavia
was forced to surrender, and in eighteen days, Greece also
had yielded. British troops in Greece were hastily evacuat-
ed by ships of the British fleet.

This Axis victory was canceled out in May when the
Italian forces of Ethiopia and Somaliland surrendered to
the British armies closing around them. The British troops

in Libya, however, were bottled up in the coastal city of Tobruk by the Afrika Korps.

The treaty Germany had signed with the Soviet Union had left Hitler free to invade Poland and conquer France and wage war against Great Britain, but actually, he had always regarded the Soviet Union as Germany's major enemy. Now, with France defeated and Great Britain's forces tied down in North Africa, Hitler felt ready to deal with the Soviet Union, and on June 22, in a move that surprised the world, 120 German divisions swept into Russia.

Russian civilians digging ditches to halt the advance of German tanks against Moscow in 1941.

The leader of the Soviet Union was Joseph Stalin. Like Hitler and Mussolini, he was a complete dictator—a leader with total authority. Although he made the Soviet Union into a great world power, he was brutal and ruthless, ordering the execution and imprisonment of millions of people, and no one dared oppose him. However, he was caught by surprise by the German invasion.

Throughout June, July, and August, the German panzer divisions sped over the flat plains of western Russia making spectacular gains, capturing the cities of Minsk and Smolensk, taking 390,000 prisoners and 4,500 tanks. Despite savage Russian counterattacks, the German steam-roller thrust steadily forward, its intention the capture of the Russian capital, Moscow, which German military leaders felt sure would cause the Soviet Union to collapse.

Since the beginning of the year, the "Battle of the Atlantic" had been taking place, with the "wolf-packs" of fifteen to twenty German submarines attacking all merchant ships approaching Britain, to cut off deliveries of food and war materials. By the time of the invasion of Russia, Britain was feeling a serious pinch. The U.S. President, Franklin D. Roosevelt, believed that if Britain fell and the Axis was victorious, freedom would be in danger everywhere, and he felt that the United States should help Britain. In August he announced that American ships carrying supplies to Britain would be guarded by U.S. war-

The Allied leaders of World War II: At left, Russian Premier Joseph Stalin; below, U.S. President Franklin D. Roosevelt (seated, left) and British Prime Minister Winston Churchill.

ships which would fight any German submarines attempting an attack. This virtually made the United States a British ally.

Throughout September, the German armored divisions in Russia continued to advance, capturing more cities and taking more than a million prisoners. But in October, autumn rains turned the Russian dirt roads into trails of thick mud and the advance bogged down. On December 6, with the dreadful cold of Russian winter setting in, Russian forces launched a counter-offensive and the Germans, weakened and ill-equipped for the numbing cold, began to fall back. In Libya, too, where the British had managed to build up their forces and make a counterattack, the Afrika Korps was pulling back.

Now, an event as shocking as the German invasion of Russia took place. Because of Japan's raw aggression against China, the United States had halted the sale of all material to the Japanese Empire, including oil, which was vital to Japan's very existence. The Japanese decided that the only way they could survive would be to seize territory in the Pacific area that could provide the oil and materials they needed. But this, they knew, would mean war with the United States, whose naval power they feared. So, they determined to cripple that power, and on the morning of December 7, hundreds of Japanese planes roared up from a fleet of aircraft carriers and made a sneak bombing attack on the American naval base at Pearl Harbor, Hawaii. Three

Dazed and wounded American sailors stare at a sky full of smoke and flame
following the Japanese surprise attack on the U.S. naval base at Pearl
Harbor, Hawaii. In addition to the ships sunk and damaged in the water,
many planes at American airfields were destroyed where they stood.

U.S. battleships were sunk, five were severely damaged, and six other warships were also damaged. On December 8, President Roosevelt spoke before the U.S. Congress asking for a formal declaration of war. He called the attack "a day that would live in infamy."

Within the next few days Japanese troops invaded the British colonies of Hong Kong and Malaya, the American-controlled Philippine Islands, and the American-owned islands of Guam and Wake Island. On December 11, Germany and Italy declared war on the United States. The year ended with German troops giving ground in Russia and Libya, but with American and British forces being overwhelmed and destroyed everywhere in the Pacific area.

Three U.S. battleships (including the U.S.S. *Arizona*, below) were sunk and eleven other ships badly damaged in the Japanese bombing of Pearl Harbor.

★

THE U.S. FLEET had, indeed, been crippled by the Japanese raid on Pearl Harbor, and in January a series of battles between Japanese and U.S., British, and Dutch warships left the Japanese in total control of southeastern Pacific waters. Japanese troops swarmed almost unopposed into French Indo-China (now Viet Nam, Laos, and Kampuchea), British-ruled Burma, the Dutch East Indies (now Indonesia), and the Australia-controlled Admiralty Islands. In February, the British troops in Malaya surrendered to the Japanese; in March, the forces in the Dutch East Indies surrendered; and in May, the thousands of American troops in the Philippines were forced to surrender, while the tattered remnants of the British army in Burma retreated into India, leaving Burma in Japanese hands. Also in May, the naval Battle of the Coral Sea was fought, and although the U.S. force sank the small Japanese aircraft carrier *Shoho*, the American carrier *Lexington* went down. Things seemed bleak for the Allies in Asia and the Pacific area.

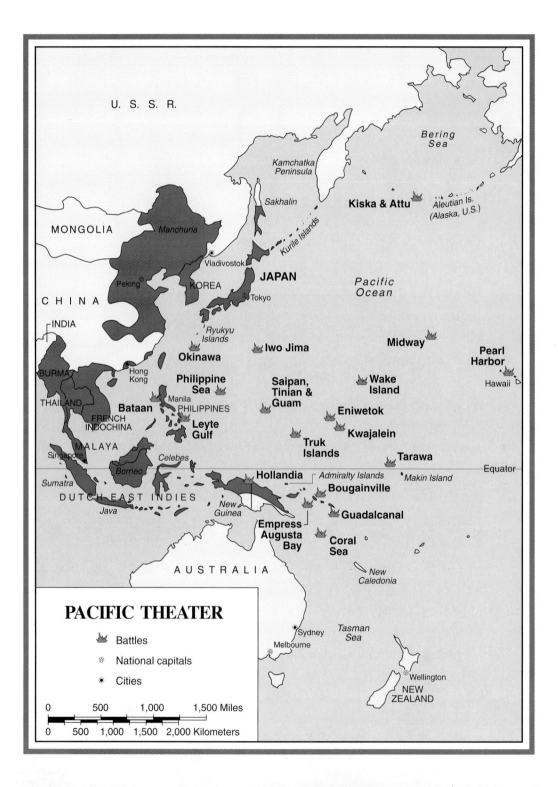

U. S. S. R.

Bering
Sea

Kamchatka
Peninsula

Sakhalin

Kiska & Attu

Aleutian Is.
(Alaska, U.S.)

MONGOLIA   Manchuria

Kurile Islands

Vladivostok

Peking   KOREA   **JAPAN**

CHINA   Tokyo

Pacific
Ocean

Midway

Pearl
Harbor

INDIA

Ryukyu
Islands

Iwo Jima

Hawaii

BURMA   Hong
Kong

Okinawa

**Philippine
Sea**

**Saipan,
Tinian &
Guam**

**Wake
Island**

THAILAND

Manila
PHILIPPINES

Bataan

FRENCH
INDOCHINA

**Leyte
Gulf**

Eniwetok

Kwajalein

MALAYA

**Truk
Islands**

Tarawa

Singapore

Celebes

Sumatra   Borneo

Hollandia   Admiralty Islands   Makin Island   Equator

DUTCH EAST INDIES   **Bougainville**

Java   New
Guinea

Guadalcanal

**Empress
Augusta
Bay**

**Coral
Sea**

AUSTRALIA   New
Caledonia

PACIFIC THEATER

Battles

National capitals

Cities

Sydney   Tasman
Sea

Melbourne

Wellington

NEW
ZEALAND

0	500	1,000	1,500 Miles

0	500	1,000	1,500	2,000 Kilometers

And they were bleak everywhere else, as well. In Russia, the German armies had halted their pullback, fought the Russian advance to a standstill, and then, reinforced by fifty-two divisions, pushed forward and drove the Russians back. In the sandy windswept desert in Libya, the British 8th Army and the Afrika Korps had been fighting a seesaw battle, but by late May the Afrika Korps was beginning to push the British back. And in the Atlantic Ocean, German submarines were now operating along the American east coast, taking a heavy toll of merchant ships.

The Japanese had now put together a plan they believed could knock the United States out of the war in the Pacific, and on June 4, Japanese naval forces attacked the vital American base of Midway Island. But the Americans had deciphered the Japanese radio code, knew about the attack, and scraped together all the ships they could, including three aircraft carriers, to fight off the Japanese forces. In a battle fought mainly between ships and airplanes, the United States lost one carrier and a destroyer, but American dive bombers sank four Japanese carriers and a cruiser. The Japanese had to call off the attack and withdraw. It was a catastrophic defeat for Japan, which, although it was not known at the time, turned the war in America's favor.

And America now went on the offensive. On August 7, a force of U.S. marines invaded several islands of the Solomons group, wiping out the Japanese defenders on two and driving those on Guadalcanal Island into hiding. From

Combat between ships and airplanes was a major feature of the war in the
Pacific in World War II. In this photo, an American ship in the waters near
Guadalcanal is being attacked by two Japanese planes, one of which has
been shot down and is plunging into the sea.

their nearest base, the Japanese launched air raids and sent small fleets of warships to attack the American invasion fleet. Throughout September and October, the Japanese managed to land small numbers of troops on Guadalcanal, and there were battles on the island as well as vicious naval battles in the waters around it. Grimly, the American forces hung on.

In Russia during this time, German and Soviet forces became locked in a titanic battle in and around the Russian city of Stalingrad (now called Volgograd), with soldiers fighting almost hand-to-hand from street to street. In North Africa, the Afrika Korps had pushed the British all the way back into Egypt, where they halted and formed a defensive line at the coastal town of El Alamein. In a battle that raged from August 31 to September 7, the Afrika Korps battered against stubborn British resistance. Finally, their tanks running short of fuel, the Axis troops fell back. The British built up their force with men and supplies brought by ships, and on October 23 lashed out in an offensive that became known as the Battle of El Alamein. By November 4, the German and Italian forces of the Afrika Korps were in full retreat.

Despite its vast operations in the Pacific area, the United States had always regarded the war against Germany as of main importance and had been building up to take part in it. Now, suddenly, on November 8, U.S. troops with some

General Dwight D. "Ike" Eisenhower commanded the U.S. and British force that invaded North Africa in 1942. He went on to become supreme commander of Allied forces in Europe, and seven years after the war he was elected 34th President of the United States.

British units, all commanded by American General Dwight D. Eisenhower (who was to become the 34th President of the United States), landed at several places on the North Africa coast and began a drive toward the French-controlled nation of Tunisia, which was the base for supplies and reinforcements for the Axis troops in North Africa.

Throughout November, numerous Japanese attempts to reinforce and supply their troops on Guadalcanal failed, whereas the American force had been built up. On November 19, Russian armies launched a double attack that surrounded the German forces in Stalingrad. Thus, the year that had begun bleakly ended on a high note for the Allies, with the Germans in serious trouble in Russia, U.S. troops on Guadalcanal preparing to mop up the remaining Japanese, and Rommel's Afrika Korps caught between two Allied armies.

FIVE
1943

★

IN NORTH AFRICA, the American invasion force was unable to reach the city of Tunis, in Tunisia, before General Rommel's Afrika Korps arrived there and linked up with other Axis troops. On February 14, Rommel made a quick attack that caught the advancing Americans by surprise and smashed through them. German tanks sped toward the American rear, threatening to capture the main supply area. But American and British reinforcements were rushed forward and managed to hold their ground, forcing the Axis troops to eventually begin pulling back. In March, Rommel attacked again, in a different direction, against the British army that had pursued him from Egypt. But the attack was easily repulsed, and now Rommel, ill and exhausted, was flown back to Germany.

The Axis situation in North Africa was now hopeless. On April 22, the Allied armies began a great offensive, thrusting the Axis forces back to a last-ditch defensive line in front of the port cities of Tunis and Bizerte. On May 6, following a titanic artillery barrage, Allied tanks rumbled forward and broke through the Axis line. American

Despite the genius of its commander, Field Marshal Erwin Rommel, the Axis army in North Africa was overwhelmed by American and British forces that closed around it in the early months of 1943. Here, infantrymen of the British 8th Army capture a German tank.

and British troops began to push into Tunis and Bizerte. With escape by sea blocked by Allied ships and planes, the Axis troops were trapped and surrendered by the hundreds of thousands. The war in North Africa was over, an Allied victory.

In Russia, the 93,000 German soldiers trapped in Stalingrad had surrendered on February 2nd, and the Russian armies had immediately begun a drive westward, retaking the German-held city of Kursk. A German counterattack brought the advance to a halt and pushed it back until sixty Russian divisions were clustered in a bulge around Kursk, caught between two German army groups. On July 5, the Germans attacked from both sides and the greatest tank battle of history began, with thousands of armored vehicles pitted against one another.

Even as this tremendous struggle of machines was taking place, the Allies struck a sudden blow at Germany's Axis partner, Italy. On July 10, the U.S. 7th Army and British 8th Army were landed from the sea on the island of Sicily, off the southern part of Italy, and began to move against the German and Italian troops there. Alarmed by this invasion, Hitler ordered his commanders in Russia to break off the Battle of Kursk and begin sending panzer divisions back to the west. As the German forces pulled away from Kursk, the Russians moved after them in a huge offensive, and in Moscow, victory bells began to ring. The Russians knew they had defeated the German invasion and began to push the panzer forces out of their country.

Above, a German soldier leaps from a burning tank in the Battle of Kursk, in Russia. Below, a sad casualty of the Allied attack on Italy: a 1,300-year-old monastery smashed to ruins by bombs.

On July 24, the Italian people deposed and imprisoned their dictator, Mussolini, and formed a new government. By mid-August Sicily was in Allied hands, and on September 3 the British 8th Army invaded southern Italy.

Five days later the new Italian government announced that it had signed an armistice with the Allies, and Italy was now out of the war. The next day the U.S. 5th Army landed at another part of Italy, farther up the coast from the British, but it met fierce resistance from German forces, which were intent on holding onto Italy to prevent the Allies from using it as a pathway up into Germany. The Germans set up a fortified line blocking Allied advance.

On November 20, U.S. forces invaded the Japanese-held Pacific islands of Makin and Tarawa, northeast of Australia. By the 23rd, all Japanese resistance had been wiped out on Makin, and on the 24th, after one of the bloodiest battles in U.S. history, Tarawa was taken. It was the plan of the American military leaders to use these islands as bases for an "island hopping" campaign, gradually moving from island to island, closer and closer to Japan itself.

China was largely occupied by Japanese troops, but part of southern China was still free, and the United States began to build air bases there, flying the planes for them over the mountains from India. By the end of 1943, American fighter planes and bombers were operating from a dozen airfields in south China, bombing Japanese bases.

Japan was now clearly on the defensive. German forces were being steadily pushed out of Russia and were barely hanging on in Italy. Germany itself was now being devastated by American and British planes, by the steady bombing of its cities, day and night, operating out of Britain.

Top, American soldiers wade through the surf toward Makin Island.
Below, U.S. marines on Tarawa fire from behind piled-up sandbags.

SIX

1944

★

IN THE FIRST MONTH of the new year Russian armies continued to advance methodically, driving the Germans out of their country. But in Italy, things were not going as well for the Allies. The 5th Army pushed against the German line with no result. On January 22, a force of 50,000 American and British troops landed from the sea on a beach behind the German line, near the town of Anzio, with the mission of moving rapidly inland to hit the Germans from behind. But a quick German counterattack pinned this force down so that it had to dig in where it was. For the next three months, the Allies were unable to move anywhere in Italy.

On February 1, U.S. troops landed on the Pacific island of Kwajalein, a large, important Japanese base. Within seven days it was captured. On the 17th, American marine and army units assaulted the island of Eniwetok, north of Kwajalein, securing it four days later. The United States now possessed a curving string of island bases within striking distance of many Japanese-occupied areas.

While one American soldier adjusts a machine gun, others dig "fox holes"
in the earth of Eniwetok Island. A "fox hole" was a pit just large and
deep enough for one or two men to take cover in.

In March, a Japanese army moved out of Burma and invaded India, but after a short advance it was fought to a standstill by British and Indian troops. In May, two Japanese armies thrust into southeastern China with the objective of capturing the American airfields there. Japan was desperately trying to break the ring that was closing around it.

In Italy, there was a sudden swirl of motion. Allied forces made a surprise assault on the German line on May 1, and by the 25th had broken through. The Germans began to pull back in retreat, with the Allied 5th Army hot on their heels.

Now, Allied forces made the greatest invasion of history. In the early morning darkness of June 6, 20,000 American and British airborne troops were dropped by parachute or landed by glider at points along the coast of Normandy, in German-occupied France, to capture key roads, towns, and bridges. From Britain, 4,000 transport ships, escorted by 600 warships, sailed across the English Channel and landed 175,000 men on the beaches of Normandy, where they launched an assault against the German fortifications strung along the coast. As if in retaliation, Hitler now unleashed a terror-weapon, the V-1 "flying bombs"—automatic pilotless aircraft loaded with explosives, which were directed against the city of London. These were the first guided missiles used in war.

In the Pacific, on June 15, U.S. marines landed on the island of Saipan, the closest point to Japan yet attacked.

Stepping out of a landing craft, American soldiers wade through shallow
water onto the beach of Normandy, France, on "D-Day," the day of the
Allied invasion of Europe. This was the biggest military invasion in history.

As if in revenge for the invasion of Europe, Hitler began using a new "terror weapon," the V-1 Robot Bomb. In this photo a V-1 is shown falling upon a town in England. The V-1 bombs, pilotless, automatically guided airplanes filled with explosives, were the first guided missiles used in warfare.

A Japanese naval fleet, hurrying to try to repulse this invasion was intercepted by the U.S. 5th Fleet, and in a day-long battle the Japanese lost three aircraft carriers and 411 planes, to 210 American planes. The Japanese withdrew.

On July 10, Soviet forces crossed the Russian border, pursuing the German armies into Poland and Finland. The Russian advance had cost the Germans more than half a million casualties and had destroyed two thousand tanks. Germany could not replace such losses, for the constant bombing of German factories and oil refineries was destroying their ability to produce new weapons and equipment.

On July 25, Allied invasion forces in France broke through the German fortifications on the coast and began pushing inland. From out of Germany leaked word that an assassination attempt had been made on Hitler by a number of German generals. The attempt had failed, and in time the generals were executed, among them Field Marshal Erwin Rommel, who was forced to take poison.

By mid-August, the German forces in France were in full retreat, and by September, with 2.1 million men now in Europe, the Allies were speeding toward the German border, where the German army was withdrawing behind the Siegfried Line, its string of fortifications. In the east, Soviet forces had reached the Vistula River, across from the city of Warsaw, and had attacked into Rumania. On September 8, Bulgaria, which had been a German ally, changed sides and declared war on Germany. It was on this same day that

Germany began using its second secret terror weapon, the V-2 rocket missile—guided missiles that killed 2,500 people in London.

Major events were also taking place in the Pacific at this time. On October 20, U.S. army troops had landed on Leyte Island in the Philippines. If the United States retook the Philippines, Japan's vital supplies of raw materials from south Asia would be cut off, so the entire Japanese fleet was sent to break up the Philippine invasion. A battle took place between Japanese and U.S. warships in the waters off Leyte that was the largest naval battle in world history. Its result was that Japan lost four aircraft carriers, three battleships, ten cruisers, eleven destroyers, and five hundred planes, to American losses of three escort (small) carriers, three destroyers, and two hundred planes. The U.S. invasion of the Philippines continued unchecked.

In December, fog and snow grounded all Allied aircraft in Belgium, and taking advantage of this, the Germans struck with a strong surprise attack against the American forces moving toward the German border. Two American divisions, caught by surprise, were shattered, but as Allied troops were rushed to the area, the German attack was halted in what became known as the Battle of the Bulge (the German attack had caused a bulge in the American line). The Germans were pushed back and Hitler's last gamble had failed. The end was now clearly in sight for both the remaining Axis powers.

Left, General George Patton commanded one of the American armies that won the Battle of the Bulge. Below, American soldiers move through the snow-filled Ardennes Forest during the battle.

SEVEN
1945:
Allied Victory

★

ON JANUARY 13, six Soviet army groups swept into eastern Germany, driving the retreating German forces before them. In France and Belgium, American and British troops were pushing toward Germany's western border. On March 7, units of the U.S. 1st Armored Division discovered a bridge over the Rhine River that the Germans had neglected to destroy, and troops of the U.S. 1st Army began to pour into Germany.

Throughout March and April, Allied forces continued to thrust into Germany from the east and west, the disintegrating German armies unable to halt them. By April 22, Soviet forces had entered the German capital, Berlin, and eight days later, with fighting raging throughout the bombed-out, rubble-strewn streets of the city, Adolf Hitler committed suicide. By May 2, the Soviet troops had wiped out all resistance in the city, and with U.S. and British armies sweeping through its western regions, Germany surrendered on May 7, ending the war in Europe.

Retreating troops of the German army had destroyed most of the bridges over the Rhine River in an attempt to hold up the American and British invasion of Germany. But a group of American soldiers discovered this overlooked bridge at the town of Remagen, and U.S. troops were soon moving across it into Germany.

The Holocaust—the murder of millions of "undesirables" (Jews, gypsies, Russians, and homosexuals) by the Nazis—was one of the greatest horrors of the war. Right, Polish Jews are rounded up and marched off to a death camp. Below left, prisoners show the effects of life under starvation conditions in a concentration camp. Below right, children in a camp in Poland are liberated by Russian troops.

On April 1, U.S. forces had invaded Japanese-held Okinawa, the main island of the Ryukus Islands group, the closest islands to Japan itself. Desperately, the Japanese struck at the invasion fleet with suicide kamikaze attacks: planes loaded with explosives and piloted by men sworn to crash-dive into targets, blowing themselves up in order to destroy American ships. Hundreds of such attacks destroyed or damaged some 402 American ships, but eventually the Japanese simply ran out of airplanes and pilots, and the kamikaze assaults ended. Meanwhile, the invasion went on, and by June 22, after fierce fighting, Okinawa was in American hands.

American planes now had many close bases to fly from, and the bombing of Japan increased, with its five major cities—Tokyo, Yokohama, Kobe, Osaka, and Nagoya— almost totally destroyed. With no air force or navy to protect it, Japan was now virtually helpless.

But it was obvious that Japan had no intention of surrendering. Its armies in China, Indo-China, Malaya, and elsewhere, would keep fighting to the last man. An invasion of Japan would be fiercely resisted. The Japanese government was arming civilians. American military leaders anticipated that as many as one million U.S. servicemen would become casualties in an invasion of Japan. U.S. President Harry Truman (who, as vice-president, had become president with the death of Roosevelt on April 12, 1945) and other government officials decided it might be necessary to use America's secret weapon, the atomic bomb, to convince Japanese military leaders that failure to surrender could cause the virtual obliteration of Japan. A call to surrender was sent to the Japanese government, with a warning about the power of the new weapon. There was no reply. On August 6, an atomic bomb was dropped on the Japanese city of Hiroshima, causing horrifying destruction and casualties. An area of 4.4 square miles(7.08 sq. km) was almost completely leveled, and between 70,000 and 80,000 people were killed.

Two days later, the Soviet Union declared war on Japan, and the next day Soviet forces invaded Manchuria, overwhelming the Japanese troops there and driving them across the Yalu River into Korea. Japan had still made no answer to the United States' call to surrender, so on August 9, a second bomb was dropped on the city of Nagasaki. As many as 40,000 people were killed.

The next day, Japan offered to surrender. On September 2, on the deck of the U.S. battleship *Missouri*, in Tokyo Bay, Japanese officials signed the surrender terms, and World War II was officially over.

It was history's most vast and terrible war. It had caused the deaths of some 50 to 55 million people, including civilians as well as members of the armed forces. Cities throughout Europe and Asia had been literally blown to rubble, and there were millions of homeless and starving refugees.

The city of Hiroshima, Japan, in ruins after the U.S. dropped the first
atomic bomb. Despite the massive death and destruction, the use of
the bomb helped bring the war to an immediate end and may have
saved at least a million more lives.

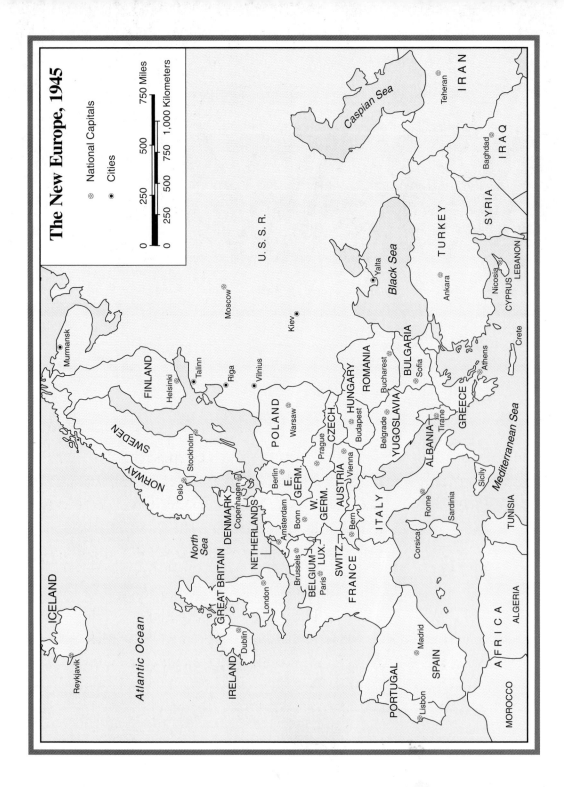

The New Europe, 1945

⊛ National Capitals

● Cities

750 Miles

250 500 750 1,000 Kilometers

0 250 500 750

0 250 500

ICELAND

Reykjavik

Atlantic Ocean

GREAT BRITAIN

IRELAND

Dublin ⊛

London ●

North Sea

NORWAY

SWEDEN

Oslo ⊛

Stockholm ⊛

DENMARK

Copenhagen ⊛

NETHERLANDS

Amsterdam ⊛

Brussels ⊛

BELGIUM

LUX.

Paris ⊛

FRANCE

SWITZ.

Bern ⊛

Bonn ⊛

W. GERM.

Berlin ⊛

E. GERM.

AUSTRIA

Vienna ⊛

FINLAND

Helsinki ⊛

Murmansk ●

Talinn ●

Riga ●

Vilnius ●

POLAND

Warsaw ⊛

CZECH.

Prague ⊛

Moscow ⊛

Kiev ●

U.S.S.R.

HUNGARY

Budapest ⊛

ROMANIA

Bucharest ⊛

YUGOSLAVIA

Belgrade ⊛

Tirane ⊛

ALBANIA

GREECE

Athens ⊛

BULGARIA

Sofia ⊛

Yalta ●

Black Sea

Caspian Sea

TURKEY

Ankara ⊛

IRAN

Teheran ⊛

IRAQ

Baghdad ⊛

SYRIA

LEBANON

CYPRUS

Nicosia ⊛

Crete

Mediterranean Sea

ITALY

Rome ⊛

Corsica

Sardinia

Sicily

TUNISIA

AFRICA

ALGERIA

MOROCCO

SPAIN

Madrid ⊛

PORTUGAL

Lisbon ⊛

A crowd gathers in the streets of Chicago as President Truman announces Japan's surrender. Millions of people joyously celebrated the news of the war's end across America.

All the Axis nations and their allies lost territory. The historic old German state of Prussia, once one of the most important nations of Europe, vanished completely, becoming part of Poland and the Soviet Union. Germany was divided into two separate nations, West Germany and East Germany, remaining that way for the next forty-five years. With Britain exhausted and nearly ruined, the British Empire quickly came apart, as India, Burma, and other possessions and colonies soon gained their independence. The United States and Soviet Union emerged as the two "superpowers" of the world, and rapidly found themselves in a "cold war" that lasted nearly half a century, during which time the world was constantly under the threat of a terrible nuclear World War III. However, it may be that the memory of the carnage and horror of World War II helped prevent, for a time at least, any more wars between major powers.

FOR FURTHER READING

Emmerich, Elsbeth, with Robert Hull. *My Childhood in Nazi Germany*. New York: Franklin Watts, 1992.

Gray, Ronald D. *Hitler & the Germans*. New York: Cambridge University Press, 1982.

Humble, Richard. *U-Boat*. New York: Franklin Watts, 1990.

Humble, Richard. *World War II Aircraft Carrier*. New York: Franklin Watts, 1989.

Isserman, Maurice. *World War II*. New York: Facts on File, 1991.

Matthews, Rupert. *Winston Churchill*. New York: Franklin Watts, 1989.

Mulvihill, Margaret. *Mussolini: And Italian Fascism*. New York: Franklin Watts, 1990.

Prager, Arthur & Emily. *World War II Resistance Stories*. New York: Dell, 1980.

Sullivan, George. *Great Escapes of World War II*. New York: Scholastic Inc., 1988.

Tames, Richard. *Anne Frank*. New York: Franklin Watts, 1989.

INDEX

ABOUT THE AUTHOR

TOM McGOWEN was born in 1927 and vividly remembers that the toys, books, and films of his childhood were heavily influenced by World War I. He grew up with an intense interest in military history, and eventually served in the U.S. Navy in World War II. In his war books for juvenile readers, he says he attempts to help readers understand that battles and campaigns were fought for a specific purpose, or strategy, and did not simply "happen."

Mr. McGowen, who lives in Norridge, Illinois, is the author of forty books, including eleven written for Franklin Watts. His most recent Franklin Watts First Book was *The Korean War.* In 1986, his book *Radioactivity: From the Curies to the Atomic Age* (Franklin Watts) was named an NSTA-CBC Outstanding Science Trade Book For Children. Mr. McGowen also won the 1990 Children's Reading Roundtable Award for Outstanding Contribution to the Field of Juvenile Literature.